Not What We V

C000264904

Born in Evesham in 1964 and a
Alistair McGowan is best known for his impressions –
winning a BAFTA for his BBC One series *The Big Impression*
in 2003. He has also worked as an actor regularly on radio,
occasionally on television and nationwide on stage (even
being nominated for an Olivier Award for his performance
as The Dentist in *Little Shop of Horrors*).

Alistair has written his own stand-up comedy through-
out his 35-year career. He also wrote the stage play *Timing*
(nominated for best new comedy in the WhatsOnStage
Awards 2009) and three Radio 4 plays about composers Erik
Satie and John Field, and the first performance of *Pygmalion*.
He wrote over half the sketches in four series of *The Big
Impression* and the book *A Matter of Life and Death* with his
former comedy partner, Ronni Ancona.

In 2015, Alistair threw himself into learning the piano
from almost a standing start and, in 2017, released *The Piano
Album* through Sony Classical – reaching number one in the
classical charts. In 2023, he set up the Ludlow Piano Festival.

This is his first collection of poetry.

*Dedicated to
my Mum, my Dad and my sister, Kay.*

ALISTAIR McGOWAN
Not What We Were Expecting

Flapjack Press

flapjackpress.co.uk

Exploring the synergy between performance and the page

Published in 2024 by Flapjack Press
Salford, Gtr Manchester
🌐 flapjackpress.co.uk · ▶ flapjackpress2520
f Flapjack Press · 𝕏 FlapjackPress

ISBN 978-1-7396231-7-3

All photographs courtesy of the author

Printed by Imprint Digital
Exeter, Devon
🌐 digital.imprint.co.uk

A UNESCO City
of Literature

northern
fiction
alliance

With thanks to all my English teachers at
Evesham High School (1978-83):
Mr Craig, Mr Griffiths, Mr Gouda and Miss Williams –
for instilling a love of poetry and language.

To all at Ledbury Poetry Festival –
for getting me performing poetry.

To Matt Holland of Swindon fame –
for believing in my writing and giving me poetry gigs.

To Sue Ablett at Evesham Festival of Words –
for unwittingly helping me rediscover the love of it!

To Henry Normal –
for inspiration and contacts.

To Paul Neads –
for all the belief, precision and help, and…

…to everyone who inspired the poems –
girlfriends, friends and strangers on trains.

CONTENTS

INTRODUCTION

In late 1982, I met a young girl on a train going from Cheltenham to York.

Quite by chance, Franny and I found ourselves sitting opposite each other heading to the same destination, for the same reason: we were both thinking of doing an English Literature degree at York University.

I'd chosen English because, a couple of months before, I'd heard Michael Palin, on *Desert Island Discs* tell Roy Plomley that he'd chosen to 'read' English at University because it was the subject with the fewest prescribed hours of lectures and so it would give him more chance to think about what he really wanted to do with his life.

I thought I'd do English for the same reason. Franny, however, was soaked in literature.

On the journey, she even read me a poem that she had written about the Falklands War and the death of Colonel H. Jones. I'd never known anyone actually write a poem before. And this was a very impressive poem.

I immediately felt out of my depth and began to think that English (poetry, especially) wasn't for football-loving, Worcester-shire boys like me.

I ended up at Leeds University – still studying English – but when tutor Richard Brown took a detour into Larkin one morning, I felt so lost (having never studied, read or really even heard of Larkin – unlike all my fellow students) that I wrote my first poem in despair and anger as he seminar-ed away. It felt good![1]

I wrote a further handful of poems while still at University: inspired stylistically more by Dylan Thomas' prose-style than anything else.

I still hadn't read any Larkin by the time I left Leeds and went on to study acting at The Guildhall School of Music and

Drama in London. After just a few weeks there, my three-year Uni relationship ended. I found great solace in poetic out-pourings – all of which I still have and most of which are totally embarrassing.[2]

When I left drama school in 1989, I started work on the stand-up comedy circuit – small and impossibly smoky rooms in pubs and clubs in and around London, mainly.

There were several 'performance poets' about then. What they did always attracted me. The laughs seemed to come more easily. The expected rhyme and the rhythm seemed to thrill an audience in a totally different way to a regular joke.

And I loved the way puns could get laughs rather than groans in the hands of skilled poets.

Whenever I saw that I was on the bill with John Hegley or Henry Normal, my heart soared.

John was a master of timing and the tortured rhyme. Henry was able to mix short and often very rude verses with sudden pierce-your-heart poems about love.

So, I started to write some funny poems – largely in their style. I soon had enough (just) to do a few poetry nights – with impressions in between to keep the audience happy and to give myself some certainty.

After doing poetry festivals in Swindon, Manchester and Ledbury (and finally being brave enough to throw in the odd 'serious' poem), I was often asked, afterwards, if I was published.

So, I tried a few big publishing houses – and some smaller ones – but got knocked back by all of them. Sometimes before I'd sent them anything; sometimes afterwards. I wasn't sure which was worse.

So, the poetry sat in a folder for 20 years – occasionally being shyly added to.

Until now. After performing a few of my own, dusty poems as part of poetry events in Ludlow and Evesham in 2023, I was surprised at how well they were received and how moving I – and the audience – found them, twenty, thirty and forty years on.

A chance reacquaintance with Henry Normal led me to Flapjack Press and, after a long and lonely trip down Memory Lane, collating and editing, here they are.

Some comic, some romantic, some personal – and several which are snapshots of people and incidents met or seen, fleetingly. Often on trains. (I've never driven a car.)

I was amazed who and what the snapshots brought back. And any resemblance to actual persons living or dead is entirely intentional.

And, the title?

It was what two happy punters said to me after the event in Evesham. Even though it was billed as 'poems', they said, "That wasn't what we were expecting: poetry. But it was good. Keep writing!" Their surprised enjoyment gave me the confidence to bring these poems out of their cosy folder and into the light.

It's amazing what a little belief from someone else can do!

Oh, and my fellow traveller on that train to York, in 1982? She went to Cambridge University to 'read' English and became a very successful writer.[3]

Alistair McGowan
March 2024

[1] The poem didn't make it into the collection.

[2] Some of these poems did. (We are still friends.)

[3] Franny Moyle: *Desperate Romantics, Constance, Turner*, etc.

Not What We Were Expecting

THE GREY AREA
2023

Out for a day
In Hay-on-Wye
I go to buy a book
In the abundance of shops
Selling old and new, adjacent.

Scanning the tight spines,
My eyes light on you,
Old friend. It's six years
Since you died. "Or
Six years since I lived,"
You'd say.

I prise you
From between your neighbours
(Whom no doubt you hate):
The Grey Area
– Sean Hughes.

You, in your pretty phase,
Look up at me anew:
A sad smile tightens my mouth
As my heart opens.

I flick through a page or two
And see your 30 years old
26-year-old's thoughts
On life and death
And Crystal Palace:
Some in prose, some in verse,
Often comic, often bleak,

Amused and angry,
Seeking love – and usually,
Unusually,
Choosing the more romantic solitude –
It's you. All over.
Glad all over.
Sad. All over.

I shake my head
And move to put you back, snug
Among the others –
And can't.
I can't.
I've brought you back to life
And cannot now consign you
To another dusty death.

I take you to the counter:
"Oh, yes. He was good, wasn't he?
What happened to him?"

"He died."
"I didn't know."
"Yes.
Yes, I knew him once. Well,
Sort of. As much as he'd allow."

"Do you want a bag?"
"No.
No."

I carry you round Hay.
We go to a café,
Browse more bookshops.

I take you home
And read your voice that night,
And the next night.
And the next.
And then decide not
To read on to the end –
Not to finish your book of random thoughts
On life, on death, on Crystal Palace –
So that you'll always have
Something more
To say to me, my friend.

A LITTLE STORY, IN A GARDEN CENTRE CAFÉ
2023

"Can I tell you a little story about myself?" he says,
Suddenly turning to us
At the next table
As his wife goes to get some butter
For their scones.

"I went to Africa once.
With the Army.
In my National Service.
You had to do it, didn't you?
And I went up a big mountain.
'Kilimanjaro', it were called.
And there was snow on the top."

That's it.
There's no more to the story.
For him, that is enough:
Perhaps all
He can recall.

His wife returns,
Unaware he's spoken to the strangers next to him
But clearly seeing the coming mountain of care before her,
Snow on the top.

BACK IN THE DAY...
2021

I don't say 'gotten',
I still say 'got';

I say someone's 'attractive'
Not that they're 'hot';

I use a decimal 'point'
And never a 'spot';

I say 'in the old days' like we did in the old days
Not 'back in the day' like they all do today;
I still say 'Hello'
And never say 'Hey!';

I watch a tennis 'match' not a 'match-up'
And a mixture's a 'mixture' to me, not a 'mash up';

In a restaurant, I say 'Can I please have...?'
Not 'Can I get a...?'

And why say you're excited 'for'
When excited 'about' is better?

I go for a 'walk' and never a 'hike',
I say that 'I said' not 'And I was like...' (*Aaaaaaaaaarrgghh!*)

I still talk of 'lorries' and not 'trucks'.
Just what the... hell
Is happening to us?

And when things happen to me,
They happen to me 'from the start'
Not 'from the get go' –
You can see, I find it hard to let go.

I'm old-fashioned 'I suppose'
(I don't 'guess')
And I don't say 'uh-huh',
I simply say 'yes'.

I have 'lots of' these examples –
And not 'a bunch';
So: I have my 'suspicions'
And never 'a hunch';
I get 'goosepimples' not 'goosebumps';
I don't wear 'sneakers', I still wear 'pumps';

Things 'impact upon' me,
They don't just 'impact me';

I don't have a 'gut',
I've a 'digestive tract', me;
I can't call girls 'guys'
'cos 'guys' are all male in my old eyes;

I say 'once' not 'one time'
And 'often' is always 'often' and never 'oftentimes';
I go to matinees '*on* Saturdays'
Not 'matinees Saturdays'.

I'll 'pop in'; I…
Won't 'swing by
Your hood'.

And when asked how I am, I never say, 'I'm good!'
No! I'm from the West Midlands and just say, 'Yeah, not bad';
How I wish this new language was all just a fad.

But I don't get 'pissed' about this stuff –
No! I get properly 'pissed *off*'!

I *won't* say 'the ocean' when I've always said 'the sea'
And a biscuit's a 'biscuit' not a 'cookie' to me;

My 'sis' is still my 'sister'
And I just *can't* say 'barista';
I *won't* go to 'stores', I go to 'shops' –
And why use 'periods' when there are still 'full stops'?

I wear 'trousers' not 'pants'!
And, as for ants,
They are 'insects' to me and not 'bugs'
And, well before Covid, I did not do 'group hugs'.

So, I ask 'where we are' with all this
Not 'where we're at';

And I don't say 'plus'
I say 'and'
And that's that!

Oh! And I refuse? To do up-speak? Because I wish?
English people? Still wanted? To sound…?
English!

ON BEING 59
2024

I watch BBC One
And don't see people who look like me any more.
I go to London
And don't see people who look like me any more.
I watch football matches on TV
And don't see players who look like me
Or anyone in the crowd who looks like me any more.

I go window shopping
And don't see mannequins
Pretending to be people who dress like me any more.

I go to France
Where I used to see people
Who made me want to look like them
And don't see anyone who makes me want to look like them
Any more.

I sit on the train and don't see people who:
Use a handkerchief like me or
Eat neatly like me or
Talk quietly like me or
Who read a newspaper like me or
Look out of the window like me or
Ask, 'Is anyone sitting here?' like me
Any more.

In the street
I don't see girls who wear make-up like the girls
Who made me want to see more of them any more.

I go to the theatre
And don't see characters in plays like me or
Actors on stage who speak like me or
Who even act like me any more.

I listen to the radio
And rarely hear anyone who sounds like me – even on 3 or 4 –
Any more.

I stop at the motorway services
And don't see drivers who look like me.
Or passengers who look like me.
And I see no staff who look like me (or even *at* me)
Any more.

Then
Safely
At home,
I look in the mirror –
And see someone who doesn't look like me any more.

JEFF STELLING POEM
2011

Oh, Jeff Stelling
You are compelling!
If there is football news to tell,
You do the telling.

Your voice is loud and keen
But always stops a fraction short of yelling.
Bravo, Jeff Stelling!

You make a goal for Liverpool at Stoke
No bigger than a goal at non-league Welling.
Fair play, Jeff Stelling.

You know endless facts and all the stats
And tell us just how games are unrav-elling –
Thanks, Mister Stelling.

You know who Accrington will keep
And who they might, come January, consider selling,
Oh, Jeff, Jeff Stelling.

Your diction's always great at speed,
Your grammar too and so I'm sure's your spelling,
J.E.F.F.
Stelling.

You do 'live' matches too;
We all see you
At everything excelling.

If you had sniffer dogs
They'd be the best at smelling.
Woof, woof, Jeff Stelling!

And when Phil Thompson starts to spar with Merse
And things so quickly go from bad to worse
And there's a major row to quell
We know we can rely on you
To do the quelling.
Phew-ee, Jeff Stelling.

Even in French, at school,
In Hartlepool,
When you all did the '*Je m'appelle*-ing',
You'd follow it by saying 'Geoffroi Stelling' –
Tres bien, Jeff Stelling!

But when the summer comes and football stops
What do you do, Jeff Stelling?

I hear you put your flippers on,
Your swimming trunks and mask
And go snor-kelling.

MICHAEL GOVE

2012

Michael Gove
Is a 'Glove' without an 'L',

Michael Gove
Is 'Love' with a 'G',

Michael Gove
Is a 'Grove' without an 'R',

Michael Gove
Is 'Gore' with a 'V',

Michael Gove
Is 'Give' with an 'O',
Michael Gove is an odd so and so,

Michael Gove
Is 'Gov' with an 'E' on,

And Michael Gove, it seems,
Will never quite be
Michael Gone.

BECOMING DAD
1999

I am becoming my father
Even though I'd rather
Not.

I find myself looking at M&S cardies
And saying, "No-one makes films now like Laurel and Hardy's."
I've got his lines around my eyes,
I've started to like the jelly in pork pies,
And when I sit
I emit
Involuntary sighs.

My hair is thinning – if it hasn't 'thun' –
And I don't care who's winning or who's won
The age-old battle for Number 10
'cos nothing really changes when
A new P.M. is chosen.

His hair is growing from my nose 'n'
His hair is growing on my hands –
I like local radio and enjoy brass bands.

I don't want to go on motorways ever,
I say, "I'll do it in five minutes," when I mean "Never";
I say, "I'm just going to the smallest room,"
When I mean: "I'm just going to the toilet for half an hour with
    a cup of tea, a pipe, a newspaper, *The Reader's Digest* and I
    wouldn't go in there for a long time afterwards if I were
    you…"

I get annoyed by bad grammar and spelling;
I think up bad puns that are not worth the telling.

I feel the pace of life in the city,
I've started to think Carol Vorderman's pretty
And last week, I thought,
"Joan Bakewell's not bad!"

I am my Dad!

HIGHLAND FLING
2024

I had a Scottish girlfriend:
Our love life was on the rocks.
When I last went up to see her,
I found she'd changed all the lochs.

HUMBLE BRAG
2024

I never really like to boast
But, aged 22 at most,
I directed Sir Anthony Hopkins
In the theatre.

I remember
Even now
How I said to him –
With great insight –
"Stalls D2, sir?
Yeah. It's just down there, on the right."

SUFFIXES
1996

You can tell a person's class
By the suffixes they use:

The upper classes tend to '-ers'
So: Twickers, Blowers, Tuffers;

The middle classes stick to '-e'
Like 'footie', 'biccie', Timmy;

For the upper working classes, just add '-o'
For Atko, Jacko, Beardo;

The lower working classes? They'll use '-az' or '-azza'
As in Naz or Waz – or Gazza, Shazza, Dazza;

While Italians think 'a suffix'
Is a county next to 'a-Kent'.

LISTS
2000

I like lists.
Lists make me feel:

a. organised
b. complete
c. neat

When they are drawn up,
everything set out,
completing any of the tasks
on my lists
and crossing them off
fills me with:

a. satisfaction
b. serotonin
c. hope

Even with music
I prefer not to hear:

a. U2's
b. Coldplay's
c. Green Day's
d. Mozart's
e. Beethoven's

but F. Liszt's.

MALE BONDING

1999

I worry I don't have more male friends for:

Going to football,
Staying up late with,
Playing cards and bantering,
Buying 'rounds' and cadging 'smokes',

For looking at girls
And moaning about women

And arguing with over nothing –
I'm missing out.

But then again,
After half past ten,
Most men
Can't tell the difference
Between a toilet
And a doorway.

ON THE BLIND SIDE
1993

I went to Luton
With John Hegley
On the Bedford train.

I went to Luton
With John Hegley
In torrential rain.

The football match
We went to see
Was postponed
At ten to three.

Our football appetites unsated,
We waited
With others similarly let down
For the first train back to London town.

Further along the long Platform Four,
I saw two men in black and orange scarves
Without their other halves,
But with white sticks at their side.

I whispered to John,
"Look, John, they've been denied
The opportunity
Not to see
The game…"

And John said,
"Are you going to make that into a poem
Or am I?"

LITTLE THINGS
2004

"It's the little things you miss," they say.
So: the lunch platters, the salads,
Finding things in the papers that you say we should go and see
That we don't go and see;
Coming home separately,
Hearing the cab draw up
And anticipating the coming warmth;
Sharing the daily irritations
That no-one else should hear –
Holding.

The awkward two minutes on the phone with your Dad,
Watching you water the garden in your white trousers;
Your secret scars that so few know;
Your bare feet on the low table,
Half-watching Jools Holland
And wanting to go to bed.
And going to bed.
Your smell.
The little things:
Letting you know that I may be a bit late,
Pretending to like all your clothes,
Seeing you cry (when it wasn't my fault) and
Holding.

Little things:
Those raised eyebrows that said 'I want you',
Seeing you rinse your hair, so proud;
Watching you rub your lips together
'Like ladies do'
To look beautiful and stay beautiful and taste beautiful;

Hearing you order
"Just a peppermint tea, please," in restaurants,
Seeing you in the bath
So silent and so still,
You asking me what words meant,
Me saying, "What's the context?"
Sitting clumsily together...

Holding on.

LADY OF THE STAMP
2001

On her twin-set way to Manchester,
Powdered, and planted opposite me,
She sits behind her blue glasses
Under her blue case
And reads her *Woman's Weekly*.
It's soon finished – "Not as good as it was."
Nothing is
Now.

She starts to smile, warmly,
At the three of us around her
In the hope of polite conversation –
My tight-lipped smile condemns me with the rest.

An eager *Virgin* guard passes
In a fading, red-striped, nylon shirt –
'Gay' to us and 'smelling nice' to her –
And hands out survey cards
To contemptuous glances from
Those on phones, in books or under broadsheets.

She picks hers up – "What's this?" – and keenly takes
A favourite pen from her brass-clasped bag,
Smelling of home and old hair.

She gives due thought to each new answer –
Passing comment and passing time – then
Finishes with relief and a little disappointment.

With a noisy smile
She unclasps the bald brass of her bag again
And finds, within her barely hidden purse,
A stamp –
And licks
And sticks it
On.
All done.
"There!"

The guard returns, bug-eyed, neatly, sweetly collecting:
"Any finished cards?"
She, alone, proudly hands hers over.

"Oh, you've put a stamp on it, love."
"Yes!"
"Well, I just collect it you see. Or
It's postage-paid at your destination."
"Oh no! Oh … no!"

"Sorry."
"And I thought I was being so good."
But there's nothing to be done.

"I've wasted a stamp now," she tells me.
"And I thought I was being so clever."
We do our tight-lipped smiles back.
"23 pence!"

I wonder whether to offer her the money
But fear she'll take offence.
"And I thought I was being so organised!"
Close to tears at her folly.

She looks through the window,
Seeing her old self, half-reflected
In the half-light,
Cursing her stupidity with a sigh.

I offer to buy her tea –
"But you'll want some money…
…Well, that's very kind of you."

As I queue, I comfort myself
That on her arrival,
Throughout her stay,
She has, at least, a new tale to tell
To kith and kin
And anyone else not really listening.

"I felt so stupid!
And I didn't need to put it on at all, you see."

The Lady of the Stamp.

HOARDINGS
2001

After many years
Of cycling past,
Today,
I finally notice,
After a storm,
Behind a big roundabout
In busy Wandsworth,
A wonderful wilderness by the river:
Tall shrubs, long grasses, young trees (self-set)
And wildflowers –
Usually hidden behind a blown-apart square
Of garish, plywood hoardings
Advertising:
Pleasures and speed,
Holidays and sugary delights,
Foreign beers and plastic comforts
On the giant boards.
And I think,
"Normally,
I can't see the trees for the wood."

URINE THE WEST END
2000

And so I've finally made it into London's
West End!
'Theatreland!'

I came here from Evesham, a dreaming boy,
On eggy coach trips with Mum's keen amateurs
And watched Tom Conti, David Essex,
Saw *Cats* in its first week; *The Mousetrap* in its twenty-seventh year,
Marvelled at the capital excitement of an overture
And endured the plastic and pipe-smoke journeys home,
Full of darkling nylon chatter and tipsy ladies'
Middle-aged laughter,
Nodding heads and dribbling chins –
"Not home 'til one! Half past *if* we do a toilet stop at Oxford.
Up to you!"

Then, a drama student, a step closer to my heaven,
I somehow paid for girlfriends
In the Gods
And learnt, from on high, the tricks of the trade –
Though my flatmate's over-elocuted mother thought
I was, for three years, studying percussion:
"A 'drarmer' student? Hoping to be a 'drarmer'?
Well, isn't that lovely?"

After below-average panto in Worcester
And a low-key tour of Suffolk,
The West End dream receded
With my hairline.
Other work came in, we know,
On TV and on radio

But London's theatres
Gleamed and shone
And, year on year, ignored me.

Only now, a decade on,
Do I have my first West End part –
In *Art!* – with all the trimmings!
Flowers in my dressing room,
Champagne in the fridge,
Cards on the mirror,
There are posters for us, of us, on the tube
And names in broadsheet papers:
Colin Buchanan,
Sean Hughes
And Me –
In Yasmina Reza's *Art*.

On our first night,
My first night,
At last,
I lean from 'number one' dressing room's rattling sash-window
To hear the lifting,
Lilting
Buzz
Of theatregoers' chatter –
That coach party thrill
Still reaches me, three floors up – three decades on.
And from London's hot, stained, summer pavements,
Something else –
Something… stronger:
The sickly reek of old and beery wee.

Ah – the sweet smell of success!

BAD TRIPS

1996

I don't like to go travelling
'cos I've had some bad trips:

I went to Seattle
But Attle was out;

I went to Sienna
But Enna had gone;

I went to Sea World
But it was full of animals taken from their natural habitats which
we are busy polluting and pillaging… stuck in small glass tanks,
looking sad.

THE CHECKLIST
1997

Every day I must:
    shave (probably)
    clean my teeth (twice)
    eat five portions of fresh fruit or vegetables
    drink eight pints of water (do they mean water or just liquid?)

    do my back exercises
    do my voice exercises
    do my piano exercises
    record my expenses for the taxman (bollocks to that)

    clean my lenses
    think about de-proteinising my lenses
    shower (or at least wash where it matters)

    change my socks
    change my pants
    water the plants
    water the garden (in summer)
    feed the cat
    water the cat (all year round)
    stroke the cat (it's relaxing)
    read a quality newspaper (got to stay informed)
    watch the news at 6 or 10 (so I understand what's in the paper)

    have eight hours sleep
    increase my heart rate for 20 minutes
    eat Marmite
    apply various creams to various parts of my body to treat
    or prevent various ailments (if symptoms persist consult a
        doctor)

improve my mind
think about sex every 20 seconds (because I'm a man)

evacuate my bowels (to Kent)

put my clothes away
tidy up
load the dishwasher
take cod liver oil
unload the dishwasher
make the bed
think about how rarely I go to the theatre
not worry about the little things in life...

And today my dentist tells me I must floss every night:
"It'll only take five minutes."

When do I get the time?!

ODE TO MICHELLE PFEIFFER
1996

When Michelle Pfeiffer goes to the loo,
She doesn't make a noise like me and you;
The truth of the matter is, you see,
Michelle Pfeiffer has a silent 'P'…

GRAND DESIGNERS
1998

These Swedes, they say, are
By far
The best lifestyle people in our nation;
They're planning two stores over Cheltenham BR –
I think they're getting IKEAs
Above their station.

UNWITTING
2000

We are made aware of our 'age stage'
By the words others choose
To describe us.

From the young mouths of kind mothers:
"Go and play with that other little boy."

From under the moustaches of angry teachers:
"You boys, come away!"

From the suspicious tongues of the first publicans:
"Alright, lads…?"

From the floury lips of lunchtime shop staff:
"Yes, young man?"

From the gappy teeth of the cruel children who first say,
"Look at that man, mummy! Look at that man!"

Whose unwitting tongue will be the first to call me 'old man',
I wonder?

INFIDELITY
1986

I left my umbrella on the tube tonight.
I changed at Kennington;
It went to High Barnet (via Bank)

Unless it saw the error of my ways
And changed at Euston – hoping
To meet me back at Leicester Square –

Trying to catch my eye as I walked by
Alone and sad –
And slightly wet.

Or did some other pick it up for his?
Oh, fickle love!
Inconstant brolly!

They'll be walking in romantic parks,
Holding hand-les in the rain,
Chatting politely –
She only speaking, of course, when spoke-n too,

Opening up to him as she once did for me
And covering him with her arching care and dark mystery...

Or it could just be in the Lost Property at Baker Street.

THE NEWNESS OF EUNICE
2024

"I've got a season ticket," she tells us
Out of nowhere
From the next table,
"To all the Brighton Philharmonic concerts.
Well, there's only six a year
But this one looks good."

Do I tell her that I'm in it?

"Lots of different composers.
And I like *The Soldier's Tale*."

Do I tell her now that I play the devil?

"My friend thinks I'm silly.
I don't always know the pieces, you see.
'What if you're disappointed?' she says.
Well, I might like it; I might not.
But you don't know anything until you try it, do you?"

Do I say I'm in this Russian piece?

"I've always loved classical music.
And jazz.
I sing. I've always sung. La!
Yes. That's why I moved here:
All the theatre.
There was nothing in Devon.
Different people –
We didn't even have a labour candidate, you know –
So, I was glad to come to Brighton.
When Steve went.

I'm 80 now.
You've got to get out.
Do things.
We never had children.
I never got round to it!
Too much else to do.
And you'll never do it all.
You can't.

So much to see and hear.
Well, here.
But this should be good, tonight.
Kurt Weill – I love him – Milhaud,
And the two Stravinsky.
They mix it up so well.
That's what we want. A mixture.
Different things.
Well, I do.
But they think I'm silly.
'Eunice! How can you go
To hear things you don't know?'

I've had two glasses of wine, can you tell?
And lovely food.
I eat out a lot.
Why not?
Since Steve went,
Well, why not?
I won't need to eat for two days now.
Huge, it was!"

"We noticed.
What was it?"

"I forget. Cheese something.
Too much really.

I don't know how I managed.
I could burst!
But I can't ever leave anything;
I remember rationing, you see.

Well, I'd better get in.
It starts in an hour
And I like to soak up a bit of the atmosphere first.
Enjoy it, won't you?"

I don't tell her that I'm in it.
I don't tell her that I play the devil.
I don't tell her either that I think my mother –
Really, really wish my mother –
Could have been like her.
Why not?
If she hadn't lost the plot
And got whatever it was that she got
Until the drama
And the music
Stopped.

Why not?

She puts on her red beret
Smiles, nods a little bow
And walks away
Carrying all the widows with her.

FESTIVAL
1991

We avoided each other's hungry eyes
And gazed at moonlit orange skies.

We talked about actors,
We talked about druids –

We swapped addresses
But no bodily fluids.

HAIR LOSS IN LINCOLNSHIRE
1990

I went to Spalding
When I was balding;
And, one day, when I'm bald,
Maybe Spalding… will be Spald.

BERWICK-UPON-TWEED
2001

On a solo day out,
In Berwick-upon-Tweed,
For the first time, I think positively
Of Death.

I've found a nook, a hollow, a cove
As natural as any Wordsworth loved.

Away from the twisted town, I crossed
A field of suspicious sheep
And followed a tiny, forgotten track
Up above the wild water's edge
With the sleek and deadly railway
Close on my other side,
To where the grassy cliff has pulled itself apart
Leaving a deep but friendly 'V' of rock
On either orange side.

And halfway between the cliff top and
The thundering sea
I lie, supine, on a ledge of grass
Under a still warm sun in the huge
September sky –
The last perfect snatch of a Scottish/English summer.

Thoughts and creatures flit around my grassy den –
Swifts soar with my spirits
And a yellow bird I cannot name swoops,
Faultlessly, into his hidden home;

A red admiral kisses my shoulder
On his weightless way
To inspect the sea
That stretches out before us both.

And I think for the first time:
This is where I would be buried –
In this tiny haven I have yearned to
Touch, through a decade-and-a-half of journeys,
Silently screaming past to Scotland
To festival, to film,
And now, stopped, it feels like home –
My past, my present, my future.
I want to stay forever – surely
I could sink into the soil now.

No.
I rise up,
Get some chips
And head for the station.

And yet I know,
In treeless city streets, when all is grey,
I'll think of this place –
I'll think of this day –
My back in its grass
My head in its clouds
My soul in its birds
And it will always lift me.

WHAT MIGHT HAVE BEEN
1991

She could have been a pianist;
They all said how good she was.

She could have been a singer;
She'd had those lessons as a girl.

She could have been an actress;
"You're a natural!" they always laughed.

She could have had a life in London
And a second home in France.

She could have had money,
She could have had no cares,

She could have been happy,
She could have been
Alright.

She'd been a teacher; she'd been a mother.
She'd been a wife; she'd been a pillar
Of the local society, from which
She had watched and she had wanted.

She could have cried.

WHAT WE REMEMBER
2001

I can see her now:
Timelessly lounging, lazy-eyed
On the hot and happy bonnet
Of her Dad's white car –
Back from a week in The States,
Her long brown legs tan-talizing me
That spiky summer evening in 1982.

I can see her now:
Younger me playing idyllic tennis with another
On dusty grass by the midgy river,
Sweat soaking my back,
My brow, salting my smooth chin
As the lemonade and lime in her tilted, teenage glass
Wet her mouth
A tennis court away.

I can see her now:
She barely watched
As I played on
Distracted and attracted by her endless, sticking legs
And I longed to lay my lips where
The sun had kissed her all the week.

And now I see her:
Nineteen years on –
More years passed than had passed then –
On those Evesham tennis courts again.
She's moved back; I'm just visiting.

Our paths meet anew
On another simpler summer's eve
And, after rusty forehands and cross-court pleasantries,
I venture the memory
I have carried ever since
Of a brown and lounging girl
On a white, L-plated car, lazy-eyed:
"I can see it now! Can't you?"

She doesn't remember.

She teaches Maths now.

CYCLING
1990

I saw old England today; found it
Through a gap in a hedge in the middle of
Somewhere. It had one distant roof
And one unbroken horizon stretching
Around fields of dry gold which bronzed themselves and then
Dived into the deep blue sky
At the edge of the world;
The high summer Suffolk sun suffocated,
Longing for an ice cream and a hat,
Beat down on unfussy roads and
Tinder forests, kilning clods to left and right –
And bleached a coke can left by the one before me.

I saw old England today and met The Famous Five
Cycling in plain shorts and white, cotton shirts,
Smelling of nothing but sunlight.
And I sat on a haphazard seat
By whispering water – too tired to babble –
Where Thomas Hardy women would have rested
As they walked themselves to sunstrokes
In the mad-afternoon heat.

And I heard H.E. Bates planes
Slowly, lowly flown by the waving heroes
Of his full-breasted girls with their brown and land army arms –
And ignored the crisp bags two modern lovers had left to dance
As a car aired past in old England today.

And where are The Famous Five now?

Inside, getting computer kicks
And wondering how to lie hold of a dirty video
For their secret teenage party.
The planes overhead are not our pride now
But American jets that train for our defence
With their offensive screams.
Yet, still, dun wooden posts
Sign overgrown ways to churches and to graveyards
Where the walkers lie who walked then
And sipped from streams
That water bottles bob down now.

WHY I STOOD YOU UP
1993

I said, "Let's meet at ten to two,"
But I must have been too ten-ta-tive
'cos, when I set off to meet you,
I didn't know where you lived.

KUNG FU FIGHTING
1997

I've never been very partial
To the Chinese martial
Arts. As a kid – full of hope –
I tried Judo,
Got it badly mixed-up with Cluedo
And killed a black belt
In the library
With the rope.

OUTSIDE

1990

Today, the football ground shuts me out.
Selhurst Park, at five past three, is a green bed
Of passion, noise and life: a seething heart –
And Norwood's arterial streets now empty.

I, outside, blindly hear the roars,
Mutely see only the insides of terraced houses
Where the uncommitted
Watch afternoon films in black and white
From the static, nylon comfort of seventies' settees.

Through a too-small gap in a gate, I crane
Above the grey heads of two young boys –
Who try to banter without words –
To see the colours move inside:
Flowing red and blue, retreating yellow,
And everywhere the brightest green is trodden underfoot
By these magicians – the people's heroes and the Midlands
    villains –
The very cradle of my youth.

A whole Saturday-world lives and breathes within these
    shabby walls
And will not let me in – denied entry by empty cashpoints,
Stern turnstiles and straight gate staff –
A whole Monday-to-Friday world
That I live outside
Now cuts off my lifeline
To its weekend ways.

No lunchtime pub for me, no pints,
No loose women in tight skirts
Or mornings after nights before,
No club-to-clubbing
No beery talk of cars
And last night's telly
And how little is left in that brown and sweaty envelope after tax:
I am shut out –
And slowly know
That I don't mind.

IN THE DRY CLEANER'S
2024

"And it'll soon be May Fair, won't it?
It's more popular than anything in Ludlow, the fair;
Always was.
Been going for ever.
People went for the rides
And to win on the stalls
And to meet people
And for the music;
They don't have it so loud these days –
Not allowed!
These new ones don't get it –
They don't know how long it's been going, see.

It was so exciting; such an atmosphere! With the music.
Everyone still goes. All sorts. You see all the school uniforms.
It's where my parents met.
Everyone went hoping to find someone –
So long ago now, mind.
Both gone.
That's why it's so important
To all the locals, like me –
Proper locals.
We still goes every year, don't we, Josie?
But our Dad, he stopped going to the fair
Once he'd met our mother there.
Well, he said he didn't need to go no more..."
She looks over her glasses, with glistening eyes:
"He said he'd won his prize."

TWO TEENAGERS ON A TRAIN
1990

And did we look then as they do now:
Brown and lean, full of idealism
And love
Of life
And of each other?
Warm. Together.
Heads
Warm together,
Smelling each other's hair
And not minding the taste of sleep
On waking mouths.

Nearing the end of our teenage spell,
Bewitched, consumed by our passion for each other –
All-caring first-love – too much hair and
Too much time; we didn't think.

And will it ever come again for us
Together?
Or apart?
Constant and safe,
Legs on legs
On trains in foreign countries?

Or will we be consigned to sex on Sundays
And jealousies at dinner parties
In one-bedroom flats
With cats,
And washing drying
And only Colgate kisses
And the silence of things unsaid?

TENSE
1987

A tense flinch
With every
Tense change:

You were…
She was…
Penny used to be…

And I would…
And we were…
And still we yet might be.

But we aren't.
She isn't.
And I
Am not.

SWINDON POEM
2000

I went to college
With a Wiltshire boy;
A bit of a loner, really –
He liked to be left
To his own Devizes.

BON MOTS
1996

It is impossible
to do everything –
but all too easy
to do nothing.

CONFUSION

1991

Out together –

You said,
"I think
You think too much."

I said,
"I'm not sure –
I need to think about that."

You said
I should be more
Impulsive – like you.

Then,
When I kiss you,
Out of the blue
You say,

"I need to think
About what this means:
We should
Arrange a time to talk."

HOUSE PROUD
1993

The dust gathers in corners
That were once kept clean each week,
The daily papers lie unread
And, though Radio 2 plays on –
The teasing sound of a brighter past
Of memories and laughter –
It stays unheard,
Like the countless records that once were
Precious – scootering home from Stratford, pillion,
She'd grasped Tchaikovsky's *Romeo and Juliet* to her chest
And couldn't wait.
But now they stand, squashed with the rest,
Unwanted, long-unplayed.

Knitting needles no longer chatter
Through the early evening's television
And the happy coal fire she used to tend
And tease and poke and scrabble into life and death is
Simply gas. The furniture of five decades
Never moves around but sits, comfortably, going grey –
And even the bad case of distemper on the walls goes unvetted.

Their every meal from box or bag is shaken or unwrapped:
There's no love in the edging on that pastry
Or homegrown pride in that sweet rhubarb now.
Photos fade on walls, in albums,
Of sunny days and sideburns and her love (with hair!) jumping
Up a wall in black and white –
"We don't seem to take so many now."

And Life goes on outside.
New fashions pass the house by;
It stays untouched by all but
Time
Who lays his heavy coat of dust
On carpet, cushion
And on her very soul.

ON DISCOVERING ONE'S OWN
INTELLECTUAL SNOBBERY
1992

You had lovely blue eyes,
You had tumbling hair,
What looked like strong thighs,
An ethereal air,
Large, sexy hips,
And kissable (kissed) lips –
I could see your smooth shoulders
And the fact you were older
Suited me fine.

You bought me some wine
And the way that you smiled
Had me beguiled –
But my sap soon stopped welling
When I saw your bad spelling.

It's 'i' before 'e'
Except after 'c' –

It's not rocket 'sceince'!

OUT OF MY DEPTH
1989

You have a V-neck jumper
From Hobbs, no less.
It has a shadow of a darker 'V' around the neckline
But the rest one colour is of pure sea, clear sky blue.

Your eyes are of this same, warm hue –
A shadow of a darker eye around each iris –
That gazing on you, the enraptured eye
Sees one enticing ocean of blue
Crowned by the dark cliff-shambling rocks
Of your tumbling hair.

I see the sun of my love
Glimmer in that blue
And then come bouncing back to me;
I warm the surface of that luscious water –
Though the depths below still dark and treacherous lie –

And, longing to dive into this lagoon that is you,
I feel myself drown in the living blue –
Like Tennyson's lark after his friend's death –
And my friendly love dies
In its own self-consuming passion:
A sightless song of unheard twitterings.

MILES APART
1992

We talk small talk;
I want to say how I've missed you.

You talk of your boyfriend;
I want to say, "Leave him!"

I talk of our nights,
Want to say how I love you.

We talk for an hour;
It seems like a minute.

We say goodbye;
I want to see you.

WRITING HOME
1997

After six years together,
Sex was dying out:
It was no longer anything
To write home about.
Which was a shame –
His parents used to love those letters.

6 THINGS PEOPLE DON'T SAY
WHEN YOU'RE LOSING YOUR HAIR
1997

1. You haven't changed since you were ten!
2. Still got those boyish good looks, then.
3. New haircut – ummm, looks great!
4. You look a bit like Stallone mate.
5. You're looking really, really well!
6. Can I borrow your hair gel?

STILL LIFE
1992

The man from Coventry sat under his hat
And his fur-lined anorak,
Twitching, and talking to his watch
As he checked the Midlands by: "On schedule – almost."

Straining to communicate, "It's bucketing down out there,"
He leapt from rain to snow,
"They talk of this global warming but I don't know so much,
It's been pretty cold of late.
That's why I bought this hat, see,
'cos that Ian McCaskill told me
It was going to get colder
And now I'm that little bit older
I feel it, see, though I'm only forty. Humh!"

He didn't go to the football ground
But he remembered the magical day
When The Sky Blues paraded the Cup round Cov
Before thousands of instant, lifelong fans.

He was the boy who was always picked last
By the schoolboy pro's on the cold, wet grass
And the girls now too have left him, yellowing,
To his mother, his television friends –
"Hello, Moira. What's been happening today, my dear?" –
And to his amateur photography.

That's where he meets his 'girlies',
Where they tell him teasing tales
Of what they do, with whom and for how much.
Though he did meet Maria Whittaker once – "You've heard of her.
I prefer the models to the still life, like. Ummm."

Still life – too much like the apple-laden
Fruit bowl in mother's darkening room,
On the brown table, covered with the finest Belgian lace:
"That's how she was sold it, anyroad, by that nice fast-talking fella
From The Smoke – just after the war. Ummh."

He loves his camera – "Which didn't come cheap!" –
And his sticky lengths of celluloid
Though he's too scared to develop himself.
"Wouldn't want to, thank you!

Hey, have you seen them Page 3 calendars?
The picture quality on them is terrific!
I'm gonna see if they'll do mine.
That's why I've been to London, like,"
Tapping his envelope of secrets
And dreams; it's all he carries.

He went to Australia once
To live:
"Yeah. It didn't work out.
No, still that's when I started 'snapping', like,
So, I got something out of it… yeah."

And the world passes by outside.

"I've got a bit of shopping to do
But I'm a bit late now,
What with the train;
'arf an hour earlier and I'da bin alright.
Innit a shame? I'll have to come in tomorrow, now. Hummh."
And gone –
No questions asked –
Clutching his envelope,
His little hat protecting him
From bad weather.

00:15, THE ELEPHANT
1989

He must be eighty
And he sits with his life at his side
In someone else's laundry bag.

His eyes pushed deep in their sockets,
His head a prune in his curled and simian hand
Upon a serviette of crumpled clothes –
Half-finished bones beneath.

A gent manqué (white shoes, white socks),
He opens and shuts an *Evening Standard*;
Catching his manic reflection,
He opens and shuts
Opens and shuts
Opens and shuts
And laughs
And finds
The crossword.
Folds, bangs, settles.

He slips a betting shop pen from his coat pocket
To fill in 27 down;
"Three letters: 'Finish'…?
End."

He keeps the rest for later
And, slumping,
Disappears
Inside the dungarees
He can't remember
Being given.
He starts,

Then talks to ghostly commuters:
"Good day!
Lovely!
You too!
I say!
Good!"

Still,
On the last train to Morden,
The end of the line.

His unseen eyes close.
His head falls to his chest.
He could be dead.

SMALL TOWN
1991

And there they are:
Those old school faces!
Older now but in the same old places,
They've aged in packs here
Over unmarked years of Friday nights.

Lads remember the times together
They'd chosen to forget alone
And nudge knowingly
At a pretty blonde's fizzy entrance
For the secrets in her past.

But she hides nothing tonight,
Tottering and tugging
At a waistline hem.

Hard to believe they're married now, some,
Others divorced already – only twenty-six –
And the set still badgers itself into crawling from bath
To bar
To car
To bed.

They come out in dangerous couples
As old flames – with less hair to flicker –
Still threaten to burn
And some, with tighter trousers now, still wait
And hope that
One day…

And so another generation will come and stand,
Glass in hand,
Or sit with nervous legs
Ripping up beer mats
And folding crisp bags into pointless balls
And complain about the dumps they drink in
Once dear to the parents
They'll never fully know,
In their empty houses
Full of little dogs –
Real and china –
And ambitions
They wish they'd had
When they were young
And single
And free.

POST-HASTE
1987

The difference between missing
and kissing
is just
one letter.

HAVING A BUTCHERS
1997

In order to do something new
I went for an interview
At a charcuterie.

They asked to see my C.V.,
I offered them
My pork-folio.

DEATH ON TWO LEGS

1991 – *written on the death of Freddie Mercury*

As a boy I heard him
Singing in another room
Of 'little Jimmy', 'sheer heart attacks'
And the 'fools of the first division';
Dressing sister for school,
Washing over her in the bath on Friday night,
Somehow helping the homework
With those
Floating vocals,
Wailing guitars
And Dad-maddening drums.

As the years went by, he still came to me
On unloved others' radio sets (from Leeds to London) –
At sterile parties under red lightbulbs,
On thumping jukeboxes in salty pubs,
Clothes shop memories of a cheesecloth childhood.

And I remembered sitting with her,
Cross-legged and laughing on the bedroom floor,
Playing endless Monopoly
With a plate of *Flying Saucers* on the side
And Queen on the turntable.

One of the family, he
Helped us through illness and argument
And holidays in the sickly car
But now, no more:
The record finally finished and all
Deadly silent.

And so, this wet November morning,
On another lonely radio,
Those words reach deeper:
"When I'm gone..." he sings, prophetically.
"I sometimes wish I'd never been born at all..."
"All dead.
All dead."

My stomach burns.

And I think of her.

THE RULES OF THE GAME
2003

On cold Christmas mornings,
Almost every young year,
One present in our noisy, bed-end pillowcases
Would be a bulky board game –
Not the latest one we'd seen, excitedly,
On TV,
But another Mum had found somewhere
And thought looked… "Interesting."

"How do we play?" we asked, politely.
The rules were always written inside the lid of the box
And spoke of 'margin men' and 'deeds' and 'homes'.

One person – usually my (older) sister –
Kept the lid and told the happy family,
What we did wrong
As we went along.

So, now, in my mid-thirties,
Where love is the game,
Confused, accused
Like all the margin men
I seem to do wrong to one and all –
Friend and girl-friend, lover and 'ex':
"You can't behave like that!"
"That's not the way it's done!"
"Those aren't the rules!"
"It's not fair!"

Then, in a quiet taxi, one late night home,
I tell the patient, Irish driver my theory that
Women have the lid with love's rules on
And men only learn them
When they've made a bad move.

He seems impressed – and then says,
"I'll tell you what's on that lid, boy.
Feck all!
They just make the rules up as they go along!"

Perhaps that's why my sister
Always beat me at 'Frustration'
And I was better at 'Sorry'.

AN AUDIENCE
1990

The city sleeps – as much as cities ever do –
And a brittle silence settles
On the still streets of hillside Cork
One loveless summer.

Now the night is cool enough to stroll into
Though the day too hot for even sleep
As old Cork puts its head on its hill
Overlooking the glow of its emptying heart.

The town belongs to the taxi drivers
Chicaning home girls from the clubs –
Taken for the last ride of the night.
And the lads from the lock-in
Who passenger past cursing others
Striving to balance on the see-saw streets,
Waiting for friends who can't wait:
"Moind yer shoes now!"

They don't see me
Sleeplessly strolling,
Watching their lives fold
And unfold. All new to me and fresh this night:
Their staleness – days familiar as the beery dust
Hoovered from O'Mahony's floral by the cleaner
Who now sweats her way home past the
Squat houses of warm, breathing sleepers
And late-night musicians and readers-under-covers,

While, on high, in a nearby churchyard
The Virgin Mary powers over all,
Sagaciously bowed to a flickering candle,
Lit by a lonely soul who said, "God Bless"
When no-one said, "Goodnight."

A neon halo wired above her head,
She attracts the denizens of the night;
Cat and dog furtively sniff blue grass; moth and fly
Wing dangerously close but no insect-o-cutor this –
Eternal life not diurnal death is promised
To my soul companions.

Drawn to her,
We seek some guidance in the mazy night
But impassively she stares, hope-less,
When "Ah! Ah! Ah!
Ah!" from the steamed windows of a first car,
Second-hand orange, comes mocking ecstasy.
Groans and shouts
And grunts and moans
And screams
Of another, parked outside the playground where she used to play
And pray in pure white gloves, who, bursting, sees only Saint
Michael as her eyes bulge on half-discarded labels
And the night is covered with her satisfaction;

She fills the dreams of the young and not-so-old,
Would slake the dry frustration of man and wife,
Could ease the restlessness of the waking and the half-sleepers
And strangely comes to give me hope.

AMATEUR DRAMATICS
1991

He holds his past in her hand – smile –
And no longer schemes romance – box step –
Been through too much now:
Thirty dramatic years
Of cold snaps and heatwaves,
Tropical Heatwaves, Oklahoma, O Calcutta! and,
Tonight, Gershwin – blackout.

They used to love to learn their lines;
Now they just try and hide them
As they tell us they've got rhythm
Though it ain't necessarily so.
And they worry that the costumes show
What wasn't there before – five, six...

There's less spring in that step – ball, change –
The hair has dried
Or gone,
The eyes have shrunk;
There's an extra crack in that voice now
And though the names have stayed the same
How the lives have changed these thirty years:
Friends gone, jobs, children, wives and husbands.
This
Is all they have – no more a dream of something better.
Now just therapy – up, down, point, turn –
And smile.
Smile.
Just keep smiling.

HARRY POTTER IN THE WEST END
2024

Harry Potter and The Cursed Child
Is so long; it drives you wild.
You sit through two plays, in one day,
In two three-hour doses;
It should be called
Harry Potter and The Deep Vein Thrombosis.

IN VINO VERITAS
2024

I used to work as a waiter
In a very smart restaurant
So smart, it had two wine waiters.
One wore deodorant;
The other … didn't.

I could never tell
Which was the smellier
Somelier.

OLD FATHER TIME
1992

He stands lost, across the street –
In too-tight trousers and an anorak from another life –
Outside the pub he disappeared into,
"Just to use the toilet quickly."

And they had worried, now he's at that age
When the least delay disturbs:
"What's happened? Where's Dad?"
Some senile trip into the night?
A conversation with a long-lost
Or a new-found friend?
Or worse…

But he emerged, confused
And stands lost, across the street –
Squinting at the brightness of the night.
The man once so strong that he could sport all day:
Tennis, football, squash into his fifties –
"Best legs in town for his age!
Best in the world!"

Then, age crept and
Leapt upon him like a lion.
And now he stands
Ravaged, half-blind,
Out of breath and out of touch –
No more a player in those sporting gangs
Who play and drink
And joke and share –

Out of sight
And out of mind.
Alone.
Lost.

And his frozen family – across the street –
Watch his still fear as cars speed past unseen 'til
Too late, like shots in fogbound goalmouths
Of yore.

And she, now caring and loving
Still,
Though pride, with the legs, has gone,
Steps out dangerously close to purring tyres
And guides
Her husband.
"Now!" she calls.
And he trots over,
Apologetically,
To join them, once again
Together.

And yet a shadow remains across the street – watching.
Still.

TESCO-TASTROPHE
2024

They gave me a Bag For Life
To take my groceries home in.
Outside the 'store',
My Bag For Life tore
And I thought to myself,
"That's either a very poorly-made bag…
Or a very, very bad omen."

COUS-COUS
2024

The Cost of Living crisis
Affects us all: every woman, every man,
You and I.

Even the producers of cous-cous
Have just doubled their prices.

When asked, "Why?"
They said, "'cos, 'cos we can."

REBELLION
2024

He walks through medieval Ludlow
And the warm, spring air
Just as they're putting up the fair;
His hoodie up,
His scarf around his mouth –
Faceless,
Nameless,
Cigarette rolled and ready in his pretty hand,
A backpack thumping,
Pumping out some
Urban sounds so alien
To our life, here, between the forests
And the blue remembered hills.

And someone who's never ever heard of Shropshire
Shouts from inside his bag
About 'hatin' this hateful life'
As our Ludlow boy goes somewhere –
Nowhere –
Rebelling
And revelling in it
Past all the happy tourists
And the shoppers.

And I wonder:
Why did I never
Rebel like this?
Well, I never felt the need:
Loved (and liked) my parents,
My Dad's friends and my mother's,
Liked my town,
Played sport with others,

Was happy on my own,
Never bored
But perhaps thought boring
By the rebel horde.

What could I rebel against?
What should I rebel against?
The system seemed as good as any:
We ate, we learnt, we watched, we swam.
But I watched the shouters and the screamers then:
The Clash, The Jam, Sham 69,
I went to football matches, saw the trouble after games
    involving teams of mine,
Went to teenage clubs and discos and saw the unhappy ones
    there too –
Skulking or spoiling for a fight,
Rebelling against something
Every Friday night.
Did they even know what?

Every teenager did it – not
Seeing that they were all being
The same in trying to be different.

Their rebellion was:
'A rite of passage',
'Part of growing up',
'A phase they all go through',
'We were just the same at their age!'

So, was my rebel act
Even greater then?
Or more Orwellian?

The fact
That I rebelled against
Rebellion.

JUST VISITING
1991

When I went Home,
I did all the things I used to do:
I walked through Town, hoping I wouldn't see the rough kids
Who'd tease me for my 'arty-farty' clothes;

I went swimming
And checked all the lockers for spare 10p's,
I took shortcuts back
And looked over walls
Into over-lit lounges
As dusk fell on the gnomes
And I saw strange faces lit up
By the lightening blue of *Newsround.*

I smelt the cold
And felt the chill
Sharp on my cheeks and ears
And I thought of the orange warmth of the Belling
I'd share with the cat – soon.

As I went home, I waved at old school-friends' older parents
(Still in their new houses)
And jumped at the same, self-important dogs.
I chipped footballs back
To giggling, ruddy-faced boys with dirty knees
Who'd play 'til they could see no more;
I watched the limbs of the town
Come daily home from work in unnecessary cars
And passed through the living ghosts of schoolkids
In grudging uniforms
Still shuffling outside the school shop –

Hiding the fags
But not the smoke.

When I was home, I watched endless television
(Even *Midlands Today*),
I ate white bread
And drank C-Vit
And wondered what was for 'tea'.
I spent ages getting ready,
Looked hopefully for cleavage in *The Reader's Digest* by the toilet
And smelt Vosene on the powdery bathroom.

I came back feeling empty from a night in the pub
And I felt for my father
And I worried for my sister
And wondered how long Mum would be in hospital this time
And I lay in my old bed,
With a hot water bottle,
Frightened by Death.

SCENT

1989

Perfumes, like names, when crossed again
Still remind us of that first time we knew them:
On uncharted clothes in nervous cinemas,
On tossed, hopeful hair in small-hour kitchens,
On cherished necks under siege from careless kisses.

A mist of memory each time we pass
That smell,
Her old perfume:
The sweet taste of nights
Of strength
And love.

So, whenever we hear
This name,
That name,
Her old name
On lonely phone-ins,
Across the checkout,
In new groups
Of new faces
With new handshakes
And old smells,
We start
Again.

TELL THEM THE TRUTH ABOUT MEAT
1996

I'd like to be a vegetarian
But the linguistic conspiracy
Of the barbarian
Carnivores
Saw to that.
For, as soon as I had learnt to talk
And ask, "What's on my (plastic) plate?"
My Mum, my Dad, so sheepishly, said: "Pork."
And, not knowing any Latin, I would eat
This meat
And it was forever too late
To think of it as 'little piggy-wiggy';

I wouldn't have touched beef
As I watched *Barrier Reef*
If it had been introduced as 'moo-cow'
And I'm sure neither would you, how
Could we? Although, of course, I am
Surprised I didn't identify lamb
With *lambs*.
But perhaps that's why
Our parents, sagely, give these animals childish names like
'Baa-lambs' – as far from 'lamb' as 'ham' from 'pig':
It's all just one big,
Meaty
Euphemism.

I was older when I encountered 'posher' meat
Though still no-one reveals
That veal's
Really baby cow.

And, I avow,
I felt pretty queer
When I was told the venison I'd just had was deer.
But I was mature enough by then
Not to be caught on the hop
So I gave them
The chop.

But tell me who, in this conspiracy, thought up 'sweetbreads'?
They are very far from being 'sweets' or 'bread'.

I see now
How,
Sometimes, language
Is just 'offal'.

END OF TERM, COMEDY NIGHT
1992

Not a care in your world
You dance the year away
To the mesmeric sound
Of the Bundhu Boys, in June
And karaoke madly in drunken, sunken bars
Into the larger, small hours
Of an endless morning.

Your full hair flies,
Exulting in its final freedom,
Young breasts bop inside deferred blouses
And smooth bellies nestle and cheaply fill
Inside smartest T's and polo's
On Midsummer's Night in Cardiff.

Outside, the world is wet and disappointing;
Outside, just another bloody night
But the best years of life are here.
Cocooned.
Girls becoming women;
Boys becoming men. Slowly.
The students. In their world of hope and love.
Where every shoulder is a shoulder to cry on
And every good-looking fresher will pass this way again,
Where tea and toast will do you fine
At 4 a.m. with your oldest or your newest friend.

And how I envy you.
I, inside-outside,
Alone;

No warm wet arms
Struggling to touch as much as public will allow,
No hungry lips seeking any contact,
No teasing friends to drag me off to dance in fives and sixes
And watch the girls from the front row –
Just too dressed-up –
At sixes and at sevens.

I stand and watch – your forgotten entertainer –
And feel your warmth
And see your love
And think of my tomorrow
And remember
And remember
Dancing.

HUNSTANTON

1990

"On a clear night you can see Skegness," they say –
A pretty promontory of dancing lights and false promise –
But all is ghostly calm tonight in Sunny Hunny
Save the hissing, slapping sea
Which once destroyed the pier.

And now man has taken over:
Along the promenade, by day,
Rocky Thompson sells tooth decay,
And in wind-blasted windows, obscene mugs
Lurk like men in raincoats outside the gates
To the Scooby Doo fair.

And oh, the change within a hundred years –
From laughing aunties hitching up their bloomers
To G-string bottoms flecked with sand
Which glow on cards above the children's heads
In shops more full of rubbish than the bins.

Older folk whose days are numbered
Take each other walks to bingo halls
And unwanted kids, leashed to video games, yap
For 'one more go' and savage shadows in Palaces of Noise.

Sunny Hunny where self-caterers are well catered for
In the immobile mobile homes-not-far-from-home;
While the slightly more discerning can B&B happily
In plastic guest houses which boast
'Cool sheets, hot food and a warm welcome'
They thought you only found in Leicester.

And soon in search of false perfection
They'll dye the sea blue
And paint the grass green
Ignoring nature's warning
(Scrawled unwittingly
By the Happy Sweet and China Shop's sour owner):
'What U break U pay for'.

IN REVERSE
2024

As my bicycle and I leave the house
For our normal, unthinking ride
(Full of thinking time –
For better or for worse),
I suddenly decide
To do my ride
In reverse.

And it's a revelation!
What I always speed past on my left
I slide past on my right – and relish!
Yes, all the downhills are now ups
But the uphills are now down.
So, as I approach bends I normally curse
For the challenges I know
Will lie around them,
I laugh, knowing how
Their usual, breathless threat
Will be freewheeling pleasure for me now.

And then, I think,
"Is this not life?"
Past the midway point
Everything goes backward –
And what was hard comes easy
And what was easy, hard.

THE SPITTING IMAGE
1993

She looks and wonders why I stare
Across the tables
Through the lunch hour
As she stands
Welcoming and thanking
And looking so much like you
That I feel I talk
To you through her
That I feel I've touched you
In seeing her
As if she knows
As if she will tell you.

As if she could be you.

THE DAY WE PLAYED CROWN GREEN BOWLS
1997

We play one end
After another.

From end
To end.

And yet
This game
Is endless...

THE END
1992

Silence
In the crowded bar
Between us.

The noise all around
Of banter and office crushes,
Dares and plans and football:
All light
And fun
And hope
On Friday night.

The start of their weekend echoes around us
As we sit – silence between us –
Staring at the happy past, the empty future,
Our dream, like broken glasses, around us,
The end of our life together; our year,
'Us',
Gone.

A few words in an unlucky bar
And that's all it took;
The shaking of the heart,
The painful, frantic searching of the eyes that followed.
What now? What? Wh—?

Sobbing both, we head for the quiet of the streets
Where hate now enters the picture
For the first time – sauntering in
On the back of love.

And I don't know, I can't explain
Where love goes.

It walks past us, hand-in-hand,
It laughs out of the pub,
Squirms onto the last tube home.

"What more could I want?"
I
Don't
Know,
I say.
Something…

But love has gone;
Swallowed in his last pint,
Shut in her handbag,
Powdered onto that keen cheek.
Between us –
Silence.

I'm on stage,
In Balham,
In a hour.

EARLY MORNING
1999

Under a candlewick bedspread,
A lusty boy,
I dreamed of slowly unbuttoning blouses,
Undoing bra-straps (one-handed!),
Seeing full, firm breasts (any breasts!) uncupped,
Of hitching up
Or smoothing down
Impatient
Skirts.

And I imagined
The sound of zips between my fingers,
The peel of a stocking,
The snap and wrinkle of elastic…

But today, this
Morning, I lie and watch you
Dress –
That full, fond smile smoulders
Under your still dripping hair,
Gentle make-up lightly shining afresh
And, slowly leaving for the first time,
So at ease with strap and button,
Zip and buckle,
Your slim fingers blindly knitting,
You hide from the world
What you have shown all night to me
And I think,
This
Is pleasure,
Indeed.

THE LATE GATE
2022

We pause on our hot ride
A-top a demon hill
For a sip from a bottle of water
And find we're by a gate
At the side of the road.

We'd thought it just a handy pull-in
But now see it's a second entrance
Once added to a house
By former owners
"To save the car from pulling out
On that bad bend"
And not that long ago –
The wood is barely cracked,
The gate no more than ten years old.

A great idea once –
Lovingly planned,
So carefully chosen –
"A five-bar gate's traditional."

Perhaps they, proudly,
Cut a little ribbon then
To mark the opening
(And the closing)
Of their new way out
(And in)
Now blocked by rose bay willow herb.

Now, unloved,
Now, unwanted by newer owners

Happy to struggle out,
Further down –
On that bad bend –
Who are not so proud.

The love that chose this gate,
That hardily cut a happy gap in the thorny hedge,
That toasted the finished job
With warm champagne
In summer rain,
Now a distant not-even-memory.

The spirit flown,
That chapter closed,
This gate: their gravestone.

SPOILT DREAM
1992

When she comes back,
I'll be fit.

When she comes back,
I'll be bronzed.

When she comes back,
I'll be clean

And smooth
And ideal.

We'll meet again
And fall again
And roll passion-drenched
Throughout the night again.

When she comes back,
She'll love me.

When she comes back
With him.

CHURCHES
2018

My wife and I are not church-goers –
Until we go abroad.

There is a church
At the bottom of our road
That we never enter.

But when in France or Italy or Spain,
She'll always say, "What a lovely church!
Shall we have a look inside?"

And I agree.
And in we go.
And it takes our breath away.

And we sit on a hard pew
And watch those more devout than us
Light their candles,
Silent,
Lost in thought,
Remembering the dead,
Their dead
And praying for the living,
Heads bowed,
Unseeing.

And every time we come out,
We say, "It really makes you think
That there must be
Something,
Doesn't it?"

And then we get home to England,
Watch the latest news –
And walk past
The church
At the bottom of our road.

LINES WRITTEN ON A CUT-DOWN STREET TREE
2018

I gave you green
I gave you pink
Soaked up your rain
And cleaned your air.

I fed your bees
I housed your birds
I lined your route
I watched you go.

I felt your seasons
I stood
I watched
In sun
In snow.

I heard you laugh
I saw you age
I gave you joy for countless years –
They cut me down in seconds.

A NEW DOUBLE ACT
2024

Double acts –
We love them
And have done
All our lives:
Laurel and Hardy,
Adam and Eve,
Morecambe and Wise,
Hoddle and Waddle,
Canon and Ball,
Farrow and Ball,
Mitchell and Webb,
French and Saunders,
Harry and Paul,
Richard and Judy,
Ant and Dec,
Tyne and Wear,
The Nutties
("Giles and his wife Mary"),
Cain and Abel,
Kane and Son,
Steptoe and Son,
Lennon and McCartney,
Hall and Oates,
Anton and Erin
On tour at various venues
All around the country.

And now I meet a new double act.
The knee specialist introduces me –
"Wear and Tear,
I'm afraid."

Wear and Tear?
Where are they appearing?
They're on tour
At various joints
All around my body:
It's no laughing matter.

THE DISAPPEARING GENERATION

2023 – *In Memoriam: Brian Page, father-in-law (1932-2023)*

Brian Page knew things.

He knew a lot of things.

He knew about fossils.
He knew about classical music.
He knew about films.
He knew about ceramics.
He knew about paintings.
He knew about offal.

He knew about Premier League football.
He knew about Championship football.
He knew about League One football.
He knew about League Two football.

He knew about Trump.
He knew about plants. And ponds. And trees. And mushrooms.
He knew about wildflower meadows.
He knew about food. And where to eat it. And just how it should
    be cooked
By his wife, Margaret.

He knew how to play Schubert Impromptus on the piano
And Dohnanyi Preludes, *'mit Schwung!'*.
He knew how to write poems.
He knew how to sculpt.
He knew how to charm bulls.
He knew about old trains.
He knew about stamps. And birds. And Rupert Brooke.
He knew how to navigate his Sky box.

He knew how to order things on the internet.
He knew how things worked, old and new.

And he liked telling people what he knew,
"Have I ever told you,
I must have told you … about …?"

And there were lots of things Brian Page *didn't* know.
He didn't know how to put anything back where it came from –
Because he didn't know where things came from in the first place.

He didn't know where the kettle was.
He didn't know how to put anything in the bin.
He didn't know where the bin was.
He didn't know how to clean anything.

He didn't know that eating cold baked beans out of the tin with
    a fork was a bad look.
He didn't know which was Margaret's deaf side – in 57 years.
He didn't know that drinking condensed milk from the tin with
    a spoon was, also, a bad look.
He didn't know how to buy the correct amount of anything on
    the internet.
He didn't know how to hang up his clothes.

But
He knew how to make you laugh
And he knew how to make you cry…

Brian Page knew a lot of things;
I'm glad I knew him.

MAN UP
2024

I've never liked Motorsport; I couldn't care less.
Which is probably why
When the waitress
In the Isle of Man's
Best café said to me, "Are you here for the TTs?"
I replied, in total ignorance,
"No. I'm here for the coffee coffees."

COVID'S EARLY DAYS
2024

Some High Street chains have just begun
To close their branches, one-by-one.

One of the first to fall
Is Timpsons,

Suggesting key workers
Aren't key workers, after all.

PRIMORDIAL SOUP

2024

Dad,
I couldn't understand why your eyebrows grew out of all control
And how you couldn't see it.

I couldn't see the attraction
Of a daily cryptic crossword – shared.

I couldn't understand why your washing up got worse
Or why you wore your glasses on your shiny forehead half the
    time.

I couldn't see why things you used to live for
No longer seemed to matter

And why you did no more than 'tut' at all the bad news
(Thinking, knowing there was nothing in the wider world you
    could affect).

I didn't know why you wouldn't update your language
"And so on and so forth"
And "I beg your pardon"
And "Actually"

Or why your hands were always cold
And needed to be rubbed
Each time you stood up from your constant chair.

But now, all the same things, I do myself, actually,
And wish
That I could talk to you about it all –

Albeit briefly –
To hear your thoughts
And feel your soul again
And watch you chuckle 'til your eyes disappear

And to say that I'm sorry that 15-year-old-I was ever impatient
    with you,
Sorry that I thought less of you as there was seemingly less to
    you – I beg your pardon –
I know, now, how hard it is when your body seems
No more to be your own,
That passions lose their lustre,
That it's natural to think the world's gone mad
And, "What the bloody hell does he think he looks like?"

I know now that there is much pleasure to be had in small things:
In scratching the scab on a bald pate,
In not wearing deodorant,
In not worrying how you dress,
In picking at corns,
In being at home,
In listening to Doris Day
And Nat King Cole –
And so on and so forth.

But I will always draw the line
At *Cup-a-Soup*.

FOR EVER
1992

I want to live for ever,
Be fit for ever,
Have my hair for ever.

What is for ever?
For ever is a dream we have –
For ever.

"Alistair is famously a man of many voices but this collection of poems introduces a new one – his own; a subtle, observant, wry, sometimes funny, sometimes melancholy voice."

— *Simon Callow CBE*

"This is a collection of poems that offers such varied delights. Not surprisingly, it reflects Alistair's obsessions: from football, through theatre to comedy and now and then hints at his stellar career on stage and screen. But overall, it provides a disarmingly honest and intimate glimpse of a life. And what unites all the different tones and themes in this farrago of verse – is sheer talent. I admit, I am that girl on the train of whom the author speaks in his 'Introduction' (he admits trains feature a lot in his oeuvre). I'm slightly red-faced at his memories of our teenage friendship, delighted and undeserving of his sweet dedication, and have to say that Alistair's brilliance was apparent in the dazzling and quirky boy I initially met in the eighties, the star I bumped into a few times thereafter and the thoughtful man I rediscovered more recently. This poetry reveals all sides of his life and announces its latest fascinating iteration."

— *Franny Moyle*

"It is no surprise that writing verse comes as naturally to Alistair as pretending to be Boris Johnson. You don't get to be a great impressionist without a feel for rhythm and rhyme and pitch."

— *Sir Richard Stilgoe OBE DL*

flapjackpress.co.uk